MIDNIGHT HUES

FARHAT ALI KHAN

FRESHCODE
BOOKS

MIDNIGHT HUES

by FARHAT ALI KHAN

First Published 2020

FRESHCODE
BOOKS

Hurriyat Rd, Rajbagh, Srinagar - 190008, J&K
M: +91 9419422263 **E:** books@freshcode.in
W: https://books.freshcode.in

Contents

Acknowledgements

The only way I would begin this is by praising and thanking Allah who made it possible for me to achieve this dream of publishing my own book. Alhamdulilah. Secondly, my mother, father, sister and the most supportive man I have in my life, my brother-in-law, have all played a huge role in my life and have always motivated me to follow my dreams. This would not be possible without their love, prayers and support. My teachers who helped me grow and always believed in me that I would be successful one day. I can't thank them enough for the time and dedication they have put for me. Last but not the least, my school and college friends, who always showed up when I wanted someone and acted as my therapist too!

Midnight Hues

I lay down on my back with a cluster of candid concepts
and rationalizing my impetuous reactions.
The silent void that swallows my reality into nothing,
Makes my body delicate and my existence to a near
fraction.

I lost myself in a world like a traveler with no space;
Drowning in the darkest depth of dazzling dancers.
Hideous reality to a near beauteous death?
Seems like I now float in the infinity with no will to
search for answers.

What If I Tell You the Truth?

What if I tell you the truth
which I am uncertain of,
Will you still love me the way you loved before you heard
it
Or to when my heart moans of carrying the weight of the
cold
melting
and spatter the carpet with the tears of melancholy,
Will you still love me in spite of my differences?

And perhaps,
I will fall from the cliff of my pride if you want me to,
Or hang myself in the highest skies in shame if you want
me to,
Or be beneath the soil covering my sins if you want me
to,
I will be yours forever if
you
want me to.

I remember when I see you
when the glowing medallion in the sky blinds my eyes,
when the evergreen and magnificent trees make me

drowsy,
when my way ends when the road falls,
when the violent wind suffocates my impulsive body,

I remember when I see how undeserving I can be
and you gracefully keep me alive, and my sorrows free.

I keep moving forward to a point where the horizon ends,
My head on the floor, my broken pieces of heart and
with you,
it mends.

Pride You Are Proud Of

It's the loud shout from the thunder in the night sky,
I saw the stare in your eyes,
You were petrified
of death perhaps.
My love,
How come the love giving me a reason to breathe
cannot fight the hurricane and fumble on his feet?
While the fog of your arrogance veil the truth,
aren't your thoughts clashing and making ferocious
storms underneath?
You were the tough guy,
Strong arms, an emotional bully.
While the rain was a mercy for me,
My friend,
Perhaps it wasn't for you.
Sound of the thunder like gunshots to your ear,
And the rain hitting your face like bullets, made your
heart skip a beat and your knees shiver.
Oh, to the one who deceives people with words!
Where is the pride you are proud of?
Where is the high regards you put for yourself?
The chin you raise; big and elevated,
why is your face now as pale as the bright light of the
lightening when the sky cracked in two?

Temptation -
Is What People Called Her

Comes in Midnight with its rich black shroud of velvet
with little diamonds embedded on it,
concealing the day
as if it was hiding something
hideous or truthful.
Temptation, is what people called her perhaps.
So lost, it looked me in my eyes with a heat of desire,
Seduction isn't a sin, reassuring me while the touch of its
body gently stroking my hair.
I could feel her breathe, so close, so intimate, making me
prefer hell over heaven.
Extinguishing the fire of remorse inside me,
Guilty pleasure, said the angel on my shoulder.
While its fragrance as sweet as revenge knowing well my
resistance shakes,
"No one will know" it whispered in my ear,
Passion boiling in my blood, goosebumps all over my
skin.
It resisted a little and I couldn't bare it.
Knowing already that I've lost in the little game of here, I
gave in to the midnight figure;
"I can't continue anymore" I said while I lie down
bruised in the war of good and bad,
"No one will know" I smirked.

RED

You shower ruby colored
roses on my head
when the slashes from
the knife edged thorns
still
bleed.

Destroyer of Pleasures

I wanted my death to be poetical like the ones they present in
poems; an immortal masterpiece,
Tranquil and effortless.
But the world burning down to ash,
my life built in a moment was coming to an end.
Lights flashing on the tears of the faces around,
sirens blowing and
angels roaming around in my sight.
Is this the end I never wanted?
And is this not how it had been from the start?
Expectations crumbling down to reality and
reality hurting like the angry sun rays burning the windows of my soul,
setting my house on fire and the world on flame, nothing less
than the frightening forest fire.
I didn't want it to end like this.
No my dear self, this is not the karma,
This is the fate.
The pages dried and the pens lifted,
What has come will go someday
And as for now,
My book has reached its epilogue,
my apocalypse is today.

A Canvas of Deceit

I admire your body
like a canvas, painted with the colors
of deception,
while I think of how many other men
you stained
assuring them
it's art.

I Promise, My Love

Come here,
Tell me your catastrophic sins,
When I push my lips to meet yours, moving in unison,
soft but urgent,
When I feel every regret while I dart out my tongue to
meet yours,
When I taste all your bitter sweet lies,
When I brush my lips to yours, while I think of how
many other men you promised to stay with.

Come here,
Tell me your disastrous dreams,
When I inch you closer to me,
When my hands hold your back as you arch, begging for
more.

Tell me,
I beg of you,
For it will be our last,
While I stroke your skin, mixed of beige and bronze,
creating a perfect caramel appearance,
While tear drops from the golden eyes stain your cheeks
from the fear,
When I slowly pit you down while you beg me not to,
Grasping for air, like a man drowning in a sea.
Cloth hugging your lips firmly, eyes blood teary.
I put you six feet under the ground, covering it with sand
and pebbles,
Because if you don't belong to me, you belong to none.

And I promise mi amor,
you will be my proud kept secret
for eternal.

Catastrophe

Be wise when you start experiencing passionate feelings
for us.
We develop intriguing nourishments from the dead land
to the living
and obliterate both
with a strike
without a caution.

Wrong Choice, Perhaps?

Alas,
You picked them over me
who regarded your delicacy of the starry night
To them who oppresses you to cherish the splendid
yellow sky.
Imbeciles thinking the sun as a ray of hope in your
survival
but I am aware,
It does nothing
but blinds your overwhelming jet black eyes.

No Longer Called a Coward

I am fighting myself and all the thoughts in me,
I can't think straight and conscious blurry.
Looks like I am lost in a giant room with doors but none
to exit,
100s of people but none to fix it.

Frightened with the false fallacies,
But I will still move forward.
My forehead on the floor, ground under my knees,
I will no longer be called a coward.

I picked a dagger and decided to kill him for Him,
Eyes red teary, he begged for mercy but none to be given
to him.
Cold heart, blood on the walls and I silently stared at the
reflection of myself,
I killed a part of me for myself.

Not frightened with the false fallacies,
I have moved forward.
My forehead on the floor, ground under my knees,
I am no longer called a coward.

With Great Ease

Lifeless sky as quiet as a miah rakida,
While the silence was discomforting.
Darkness felt heavy,
And the birds didn't fly with great ease.

Frightened trees stood still not swaying it's spectacular
structures,
While the razor winds chilled the leaves to the bone.
Terror injected in their veins,
And the birds didn't chirp with great ease.

Anxious streetlights flickering like a candle and
providing a little comfort against the night,
While the tear gases made the tears flow faster than the
heartbeat.
Torched down the entire sanctuary,
But the birds' wings didn't burn down with great ease.

Museum of Strange Art

I look around the museum of ordinary people,
you caught my eye.
Unbothered with the broken spaces in your canvas,
A breathtaking representation of ablaze colors.
I look at you from far away
Realizing my worth in front of yours
Could not be compared by any stretch of imagination.
Admiring you over and over,
I couldn't help but love, so I silently fall.

Ode to My Maker

In the deepest nights,
I cry to you.
When I felt the earth crashing down on me,
you gave me the strength to carry it around,
though heavy, but easy.
But why would you do this to a sinner?
Lord, don't mistake my curiosity to questioning your
superiority.
Because my heart is as such
that when I am covered in mud and
I dip into the sea to cleanse and attain purity,
the sea perhaps gets filthy.
In your eyes, am I special?
Because all I see is
a sea so clean at large
which shows reflection of my unfaithful past.
Harrowing heartbreaks and cold hearted cries,
ripples of bitter truth over lucid lies.
But your generosity is as such
that a drop of mercy is enough for me
to bloom from the same mud where I once used to be.
The roots of compassion engraved deep within me,
richness of The nectar;
made me capable of attracting the aberrant beings.
Together we worship,
together we rise.
I stood up from my prayer; a new born again,
only to realize
there are many deaths of mine ahead,
before I leave the worldly deceit
and
close my eyes.

They Don't Deceive

Can I say I miss you without uttering a word?
Make you realize all the screams without having you
heard?
I fear to fail mine and your delicate heart,
Whether I try or not, even the right words will tear it
brutally apart.

Can I hear you appreciate without you hesitating?
After all the sacrifices I made for thee, I am the one, left,
waiting.
Waiting for when my love will get too much,
Too much for you to seek the same ears you once longed
to touch.

Can I watch while you put all those efforts for me without
having you think twice?
Writing me bitter-sweet lies on my worth; Convincing,
but at what price?
Hardly healing from the wounds that were carved so
deep in the past,
Not blaming you for them, just trying to stitch my
wounds with your words while inching my breath to its
very last.

But I feel the distant hearts, though bodies few inches
apart.
I am ready to reflect on all the shattered pieces, but
where do I start?
Made me look myself in the mirror,
I could see myself for me but why did you seem
unfamiliar?

Silence for Weakness

You confuse my silence for weakness;
An illness you compare
to a dead man's stillness -
emotionless, delicate and helpless.
You confuse it
prior to the execution
of the lovers who cherished me for my compassion and
empathy.
Don't go run in blocks lamenting about how the
destruction came without a warning,
My love, the rain sends a message of its arrival by
dominating the roofs with clouds.
My silence, calamitous,
my best attempt to flee from.
The tolerance is the calm
afore
the thunderstorm.

A Reminder for You

When you are an emotional being with a strong personality and start building boundaries, they taunt you by telling that you are too sensitive, too emotional or tend to make things too serious. Let them speak. Don't let their deviant self be catastrophic to your mind and soul. In fact, having a combination of both, only a few can master. Instead, be like the water; vulnerable and patient. Flow through the little spaces in someone's heart. Extinguish the fire of distress within them. Quench the thirst of strength in people. Don't let people's petty pleasures contaminate and shatter your heart. Side those impurities of insecurities on the sea shore and be as clear as a mirror. But, your kindness will be mistaken as being naive; so if they still don't stop poisoning you, drown them.
And remind them,
subtly,
on how oceans react when there's a sudden motion on its floor.
Tsunami; that destroys cities.

I Don't Hate You or Maybe... I Do

The pen and paper could not carry it well
but I force to write it through.
My heavy heart pleading the heavens to heal the heart of
his,
consider my poem as an apology and a warning to you.
Your existence vague that I have to pull on my
heartstrings with the melody of you and I,
To chant today about you without improvising,
eyes fuzzy but won't cry.
Not today, not anymore.
I pity the me years ago,
Hoping he would flourish from this and find the fruits of
his forbearance.
But did you sleep fine?
And ate well?
While the memories of us would neither let me sleep nor
swallow;
choked me and my body could not carry on,
The taste of your venomous words made my appetite long
gone.
Look at me now,
I prayed and carried on to believe that things will get
back to you eventually,
Making moves precisely, while I begged for peace
desperately.
Years gone by,

millions of unsaid struggles,
I have moved on finally.
But look at you now,
devastated and alone,
Thinking what would have possibly gone wrong.
You apologized but not for me
perhaps circumstances forced you to.
How? How is the question, my love?
Is this word enough to fix the holes from the hurt?
I could not come to terms with you; while you spoke, I
decided to speak little to none,
while your words pierced through my heart and left my
limbs numb.

I will Forgive You, One Day

I will forgive you,
sometime in the not so distant future,
when the wounds heal and the bleeding stops.
I will forgive you,
one day
when your actions would stop haunting me and the
phantom of my flaws vanish.
But I warn you
to pray
that I forgive you before you burn twice, with the flame
of your guilt and with the fire of Hell.
I warn you to pray
before my spirit departs from my deathbed and the
words of yours would eternally seal my heart and the
head.

Yet, We Lived

Strange, isn't it?
How we spend time like the universe owes us,
To every time we pledged to pay our past dues,
Yet, we didn't.

Strange, isn't it?
How we have the zeal to fly towards the horizon over
the powerful ocean reflecting the rich blue sky,
To every time we promised to lift a limb,
Yet, we didn't

Strange, isn't it?
How efficiently we could invest in them, around and in
ourselves,
To every time we vowed to not squander the hard
earned change on something inconsequential,
Yet, we did.

Strange, isn't it?
How we blame the planets for our misfortunes and
hardships,
To every time we disregarded the stars collapsing our
world within,
Yet, we lived.

I'm Sorry, I Could Not Save You

I'm sorry,
I'm sorry I couldn't come to save you
and maybe if I wanted to
I couldn't.
Yes, I understand that
time can be remorseless
so much so
that even if you were strangling on your nightmares and
trials
in your four walled magnificent castle,
The death will still touch your mouth forcing it to create
a pathway for your soul to depart,
pleading for another few moments, forget about a new
start.
I understand
that you are drowning in your tears,
water filing your lungs and blood pounding
your eyes,
thinking you wouldn't survive,
but you did.
I understand
that every time you heard a news not so pleasant to you,
you spared no effort to keep your feet firm on the ground
when the ground below you wasn't.
The quake in your voice, throat dried by
the heat of your prayers,
making your mouth like a parched brown

cracked land of Ethiopia.
To every time I thought of you,
like the moon changing its many phases,
I thought of every achievable way to reach you.
But I failed.
Like the stars dying after living as little shimmers of
hope in the pitch black sky,
my hopes did too without a lullaby.
It's still okay you see,
dying hopes lead to something better,
like the people making wishes upon the shooting star to
grant them something better.
If I had reached you
you wouldn't be here today.
Smiling, looking back with serenity,
Writing while reminiscing.
Assuring yourself that you made it through,
Writing and building metaphors for this poem while I
scribble it for you.

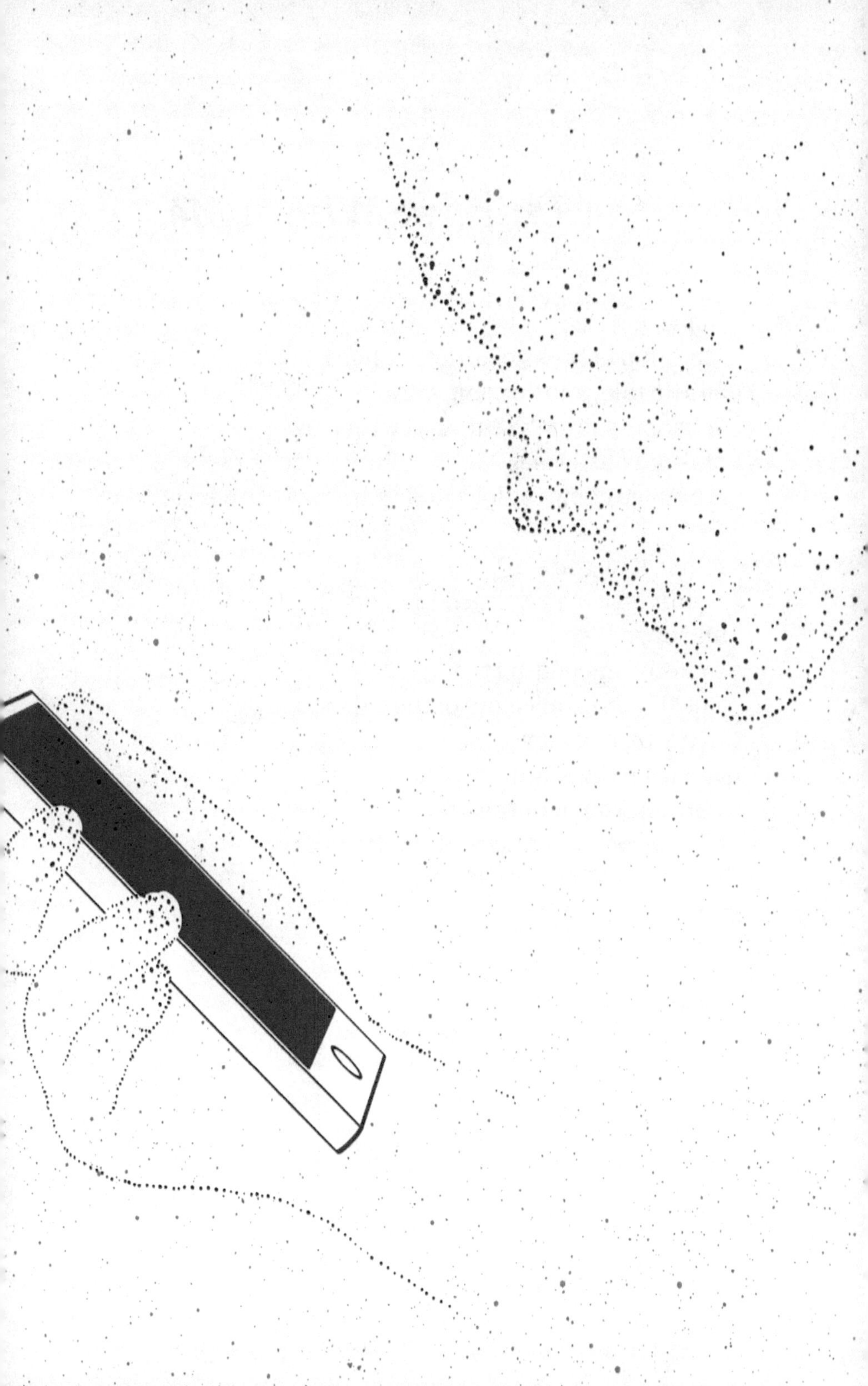

A Universe Within Me

In me, a world,
Made up of rocks of different lives,
a little tale, a little complex.
Where my mind's scattered with nerves
making out sense,
language compendious and vulnerability dense.

In me, a universe.
A universe of privileged insights
and of yours
secretly embedding them;
The flamboyant colors of the galaxy
in my pale poetry
beaming the truth.
Without you being aware,
language ponderous and emotions bare.

HELP

Help, it's making me sleepless.
Answer me, someone.
Am I adoring the image I created of you
or loving the affection I give you the way I would want
someone
to love me?
Why do I think of you before I shut my eyes,
Like a caged animal, trapped.
No longer capable to move my body due to the
excruciating pain of isolation;
love or
obsession?
Help, it's inebriating me.
Sipping a glass of water and while the water gently
touches my lips
reminding me of yours tasting like fine wine but
I do not know what's worse,
being dependent on this
or gradually falling in love with it?

All You Do Is Lay on Your Bed

Hallucinating my fears every single night
with pulse beating in my ears, blocking out all the sound
around me.
Terror sucking my breath out of my body,
Strangled and suffocating,
battle and bruises,
I die everyday.
Panting heavily and the sheets drenched in sweat,
I am not a warrior but
a survivor
is what the angels around call me.
Waking up to the sounds of my explosive crying and
afraid of the night
because of all the nightmares it has in store,
And you tell that
all I do is lay on my bed all day behind the closed door.

Pain To Poetry

I squashed down the petals of love
to a blank page,
The thorns broke down to poetry,
the sharper the edges,
the more chaotic my rhythm.

Garden of Repentance

As my forehead touches the ground,
the tears of guilt start gushing out of my eyes.
Every tear flowing, waters the flowers of forgiveness.
With every bloom, a new garden.
A new day, a fresh beginning.
Until
I decide to cut it all out again.

A Gift to Protect

Some of you are gifted. Allah has gifted some of you with the gift of loving and this love is not ordinary. It's the high intensity of it which makes it special. And Allah gave it to you only because to worship Him. Only because to praise Him, for putting your efforts for Him. He deserves the wholehearted love. Don't get surprised when that friend or a lover couldn't match the intensity of it. Because that gift was never meant to give them anyway.

Text of Enlightenment

You texted
"I love you, but you deserve better".
I sat quietly and with a sense of loss
so profound that my muscles wouldn't respond.
The dauntlessness you had
to end our
memories, our love
and us.
You changed your mind
but this,
this was different.
It was different because I didn't let my empathetic side
surmount
instead
I gazed at it for so long, so long that the torment
desensitized me for a while and with a blank expression,
"Yes, I do".
I reverted to you afore the realization hits me again.
Because I took it as a warning;
Warning to myself that
I will hurt myself if I went through with you,
Without a doubt it was wounding to end this but would be
deleterious to stay and keep on loving you.

Soulmate

I could never love anyone the way
I love you,
Our hearts adjoined, your nearness signaling
immaculate divine control in every nerve of mine.
Blood rushing through every cell of my body and
making my heart pound.
Your presence - extraterrestrial.
Every beat of my heart longing for your existence,
the same heart aches when you leave me every night,
silently from our bed.
We have a love so winsome
but there was no promise.
So while you were abandoning me,
I felt it.
My feet tingled,
my mouth tickled.
While our love felt as a mirage,
my body into nothingness.
I kissed you goodnight
with no promise of your arrival.

Colors of Hypocrisy

I question you, them and whoever involved,
Why is it you ask God to heal your heart
when you are a reason for someone's heartbreak?
Tell me,
why do you revere the sunsets?
Red, orange, pink or any extravagant shades of sky
and light
but forbid the women from wearing anything but
white?
You anticipate for the different shades of midnight for
your memories to cherish,
You sure respect the people around
but seek to cure the browns and blacks by talking
gibberish?
You appreciate the hues of ocean and how you would
swim in deep in it's elegance,
but would drown your sons and daughters if they
dared to step beyond the shore.
Realize
that every color is unique
like how seven colors blend together make white.
Just how individuals have distinctive phases,
They all contribute to the magnificent masterpiece of life.

What Are You?

When the sun sets and the moon sparkles,
Vehicles quit blasting its ear wrenching horns,
Fierce footsteps find a spot to rest and the heels tapping
on the dirty pavements stop till the early morning,
Residents going back to their houses
at 12 midnight; citizens in their bed, profound rest.
When the alcoholics and the disappointed youngsters
can not find a taxi to take them home,
Heartbroken's eyes get weary of shedding tears so it
shuts itself to sleep,
The poor searching for food hidden behind the green
color trash box and a safe shelter,
Cats and the other members of the feline family finding
a residence to shield itself from the rain pouring down
mercilessly,
When the bustling town attempts to search solace at
night since they are anxious and tired,
what are you when the city's serene and quiet?

Just Before You Sleep

Just before you sleep tonight, think about the comments
you have left under someone else's picture, the DM's that
you hide, the type of jokes you have with your friends,
the pictures that you upload, and now imagine, if you
die tonight, will your social media handles benefit you
in your grave or add more kerosene to the fire burning
already?

Bits & Pieces

Maybe the passion to build myself a new life flows from
my pen on a blank paper like a blot, splash or a stroke
forming a poem
Or perhaps,
I want to live in the lines I write, like a free verse - living
in alternate dimensions, one where the reality hurts and
one where the hurt is poetic,
my blood of all the colors except red.
Whatever the reason be, I make myself meet me in bits
and pieces of me, like a mirror scattered around; all
pieces showing a part of me- none the whole of me.
I like to believe that I narrate to myself the truth or
maybe my writings were never complete,
I think I like myself in bits more than a whole figure,
Mirror images of me in the writings that will never say
everything but something,
Something that lingers, something that carries its
essence from my parts to yours.

Maps That Lead You to Peace

The emotional scars are maps for me
for the personal wars within me,
Good vs the bad, I choose to utilize it wisely
to battle the predators of past mistakes,
to deal with the severe trauma I had to go one on one
when I was powerless and young,
to heal from the bullet holes of isolation by setting my
priorities when I was not considered to be one.
But what happens when there is a colossal armed force of
fears and insecurities?
Standing alone, stranded,
Contemplating that you are fighting a war for somebody
else and not yours.
So I took out my sword of relationships
rusted with the venom they spew
separated into two while marking a beginning of
mockery.
Giggles and insults have become the machine guns for
the bullies,
brutally harming the one before them,
not an ounce of kindness to shown who are struggling to
take a single breath in front of them.
Every soldier deserves to come home,
every scar deserves to recuperate from the stones that
were thrown.
So win
for no one but for yourself.
This is a way to find the light in the end of the tunnel,
This is a way to find the genuine goodness in life when
you embrace your scars instead of being a victim of your
past troubles.

Dear Ammi

How come you are deep beneath the earth,
but manage to come each night,
with the blemishes like the moon,
how come you are sparkling like you just bathed in the
daylight?
For what reason when the stars twinkle
it reminds me of eyes when a mother gazes with
contentment and with a not so expressible bliss at a
soldier
when the entire world claimed him
to be dead.
The moon, similar to a mother, singing a lullaby
consistently to the stars
helps me remember you,
to everytime I was comforted with my tears delicately
falling on your sleeves,
your voice calming the wildest of waves within when you
whisper - "main kahin nahi jaaungi."
Silent, in a warm and silk like land, rest, you deserve it.
But your existence never dies?
Have I gone crazy?
Or then the universe is concealing you from me?
But if the dirt is your place of residence,
then it shall be!
Let the stars that envy fall and every inch of the milky
way that is afraid to look at us collide,
The day's not so far so let the universe send a message of
reunion
to the brilliant heaven
of long lost kinship
to unite,
for all eternity.

Too Late

I cry when I wake up from a dream about you,
This was terrifying,
I am doing whatever it takes to not be
But when I see how tranquil it is,
I am anxious of falling into one until the end of time.
I am confused
What could it be that is not here?
What am I missing that I have begun to incline towards
the life after rather the existence now?
The dazzling earthy colored eyes is where I discovered
my solace,
nothing but a work of art.
Gradually teaching me how to love once more,
I attempt to bring in the messed up pieces,
Neither realizing nor understanding that she was
already far apart.

Night of Survivors

Last night, I cried a little,
A sob knowing that I am losing against death.
So don't tell me I am scared of it,
I have one
then I survive
till every day break.

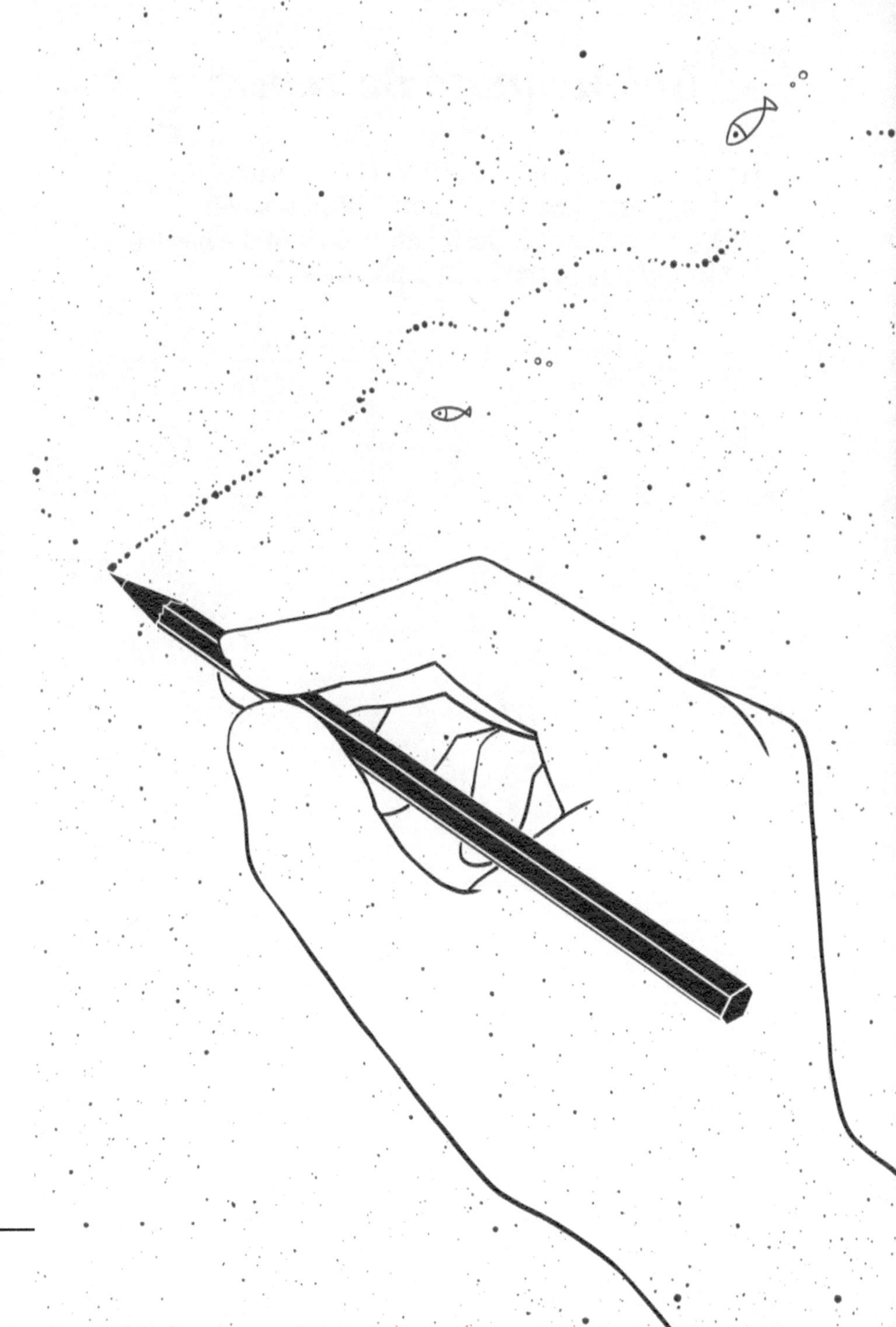

Not Meant to Be Together

I can pick the most excellent flowers from around the globe
with a phenomenal and unmistakeable smell
with petals showing the magnificence of the nature
but would reek when made a bouquet.

Let Me Write a Poem

Revenge danced on my chest
as I hymn the hurt out loud and complete
with a little sting in my heart
and the pirouette matched every beat.
Who writes when they are joyful?
I.
So let me write a poem about you,
where your love and hate rhymed.
I could have stayed with you when you cry yourself
to sleep,
But you broke down the promise of you being mine.
Who writes when they are joyful out of someone's
pain?
I.
So let me write a poem about you,
Where I turn your dialogues to rhythm.
Making sure I stress the syllable of each scar,
Perhaps that's how you portray your character on
stage by playing the victim.
Who writes when they are joyful out of someone's
pain when they snatched away their peace of mind?
I, proudly.
So let me conclude this poem about you,
Where your absence is a death to me.

Secretly burying you deep in the similes and
metaphors,
So I could publicly read you out loud pretending to
mourn over the elegy.

We often get hurt by people who don't deserve our
respect in the first place.

*(Yes, I am aware of the fact that this is not poetry or perhaps, a
good prose. But this piece is important to me. Because as far as
my memory permits, this was my first ever writing I did back
in 2014 and it was from this, I started my journey as a writer!)*

www.ingramcontent.com/pod-product-compliance
Lightning Source LLC
LaVergne TN
LVHW090022180726
843489LV00008B/2944